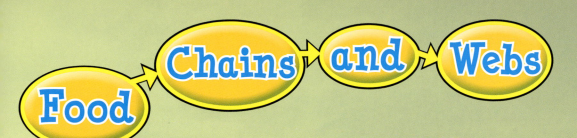

Grassland
Food Chains

Angela Royston

Raintree is an imprint of Capstone Global Library Limited, a company incorporated in England and Wales having its registered office at 7 Pilgrim Street, London, EC4V 6LB – Registered company number: 6695582

www.raintreepublishers.co.uk
myorders@raintreepublishers.co.uk

Edited by Claire Throp, Diyan Leake and Helen Cox Cannons
Designed by Joanna Malivoire and Philippa Jenkins
Original illustrations © Capstone Global Library Ltd 2014
Picture research by Elizabeth Alexander and Tracy Cummins
Production by Victoria Fitzgerald
Originated by Capstone Global Library Ltd
Printed and bound in China

ISBN 9781 4062 8421 8
18 17 16 15 14
10 9 8 7 6 5 4 3 2 1

British Library Cataloguing in Publication Data
A full catalogue record for this book is available from the British Library.

Acknowledgements
We would like to thank the following for permission to reproduce photographs: Alamy pp. 11c, 25 grass (© Danita Delimont), 13 (© Patrycja Loeppky), 14 (© Thomas Kitchin & Victoria Hurst), 16, 23b (© blickwinkel), 17c (© imagebroker), 19 (© Arco Images GmbH), 20 (© sam oakes), 21 (© fStop), 22 (© Dave Zubraski), 23a (© FLPA), 23c (© Naturfoto-Online), 24, 25 bison (© Cultura RM), 25 chicken (© Scott Camazine), 25 ferret (© All Canada Photos), 26 (© James Prout), 27 (© Ron Niebrugge), 28 (© AgStock Images, Inc.), 29 (© Dennis Frates); Getty Images pp. 8 (Magdalena Biskup Travel Photography), 9 (Tier Und Naturfotografie J und C Sohns), 25 cricket (National Geographic); Shutterstock pp. 1 (© Sam Dcruz), 4 (© summer. wu), 5 (© Andrzej Kubik), 7 (© tandemich), 10 (© John Wollwerth), 11a, 25 hawk (© Stephen Mcsweeny), 11b, 25 prairie dog (© l i g h t p o e t), 12 (© Mazzzur), 15, 25 coyote (© creative), 17a (© Peter Betts), 17b (© erichon), 18 (© Francois Loubser), 23d (© Johan van Beilen), 23e (© Smit).

Cover photograph of zebras in Tanzania reproduced with permission of Shutterstock (© Jeeri).

We would like to thank Michael Bright for his invaluable help in the preparation of this book.

Every effort has been made to contact copyright holders of material reproduced in this book. Any omissions will be rectified in subsequent printings if notice is given to the publisher.

Contents

What is a grassland? 4

Where are the grasslands? 6

What is a food chain? 8

A prairie food chain 10

Plants and the Sun 12

Animal consumers 14

A savannah food chain 16

Top predators 18

Feeding on waste 20

A meadow food chain 22

Food webs 24

Key links 26

Protecting food chains 28

Glossary 30

Find out more 31

Index 32

Some words are shown in bold, **like this**.
You can find out what they mean by
looking in the glossary.

What is a grassland?

A grassland is a vast area of land that is mostly covered by grass. Flowers grow there too, but only a few shrubs and trees.

Flowers grow on grasslands in Asia.

Elephants and zebra graze on grasslands in Africa.

Many kinds of animals live on grasslands, from huge elephants and bison to insects such as butterflies. This books looks at how grassland animals find food and survive.

Where are the grasslands?

This map shows the biggest areas of grassland in the world. Many grasslands have been taken over by farmers to grow wheat, maize and other crops.

Grasslands are marked on the map in dark green.

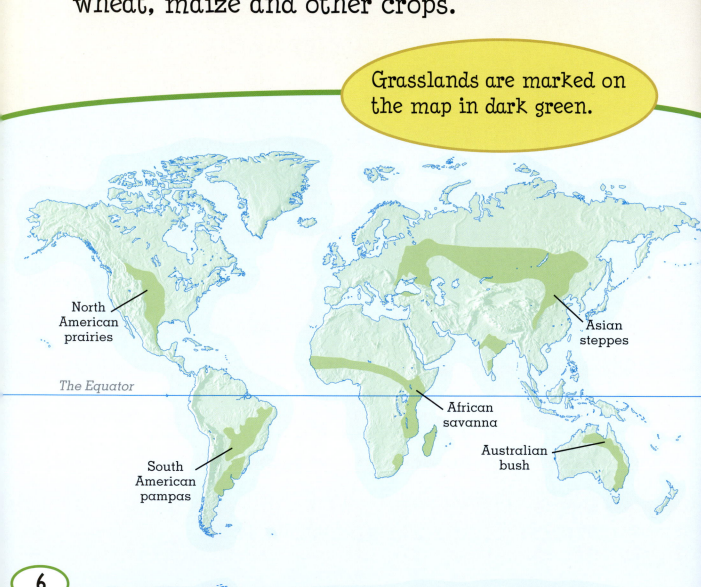

North American prairies

The Equator

South American pampas

African savanna

Asian steppes

Australian bush

Wild horses roam freely on the steppes in Mongolia.

Grasslands have different names in different parts of the world. These include prairies, pampas, steppes, savannah and bush. The coldest grasslands are the Asian steppes.

What is a food chain?

Living things need **energy** to move and to survive. Their energy comes from food.

Kangaroos need lots of energy to bound across the land.

A cheetah is the fastest runner in the world.

A **food chain** shows how plants and animals are linked by food. It also shows how energy passes from one living thing to another.

A prairie food chain

This **food chain** comes from the prairies of North America. It shows how a prairie dog is linked to the grass and to a hawk. The prairie dog eats grass to get **energy**. The hawk gets energy by eating the prairie dog. Without the grass, both animals would starve.

The prairies in South Dakota

Food chain

A hawk swoops down and grabs a prairie dog

Prairie dogs feed on grass

Grass grows on a North American prairie

Plants and the Sun

Food chains begin with plants, because all green plants make their own sugary food. Plants are called **producers**.

Some wheat grows wild on the prairies.

Sugar made in the leaves feeds the flowers.

Plants make sugar in their green leaves. Sugary liquid is taken to every part of the plant. It also feeds any animal that eats the plant.

Animal consumers

Animals are called **consumers** because they consume plants or other animals. Some animals, such as prairie dogs and many caterpillars, eat only plants. They are called **herbivores**.

A caterpillar eats leaves and grows bigger and bigger.

A coyote eats almost everything, from plants to insects and deer.

Hawks are **carnivores**, because they eat only meat from other animals. Some animals, such as coyotes, eat plants and meat. They are called **omnivores**.

A savannah food chain

Many large animals live on the African savannahs. In this **food chain**, the zebra are **herbivores** and the lions are **carnivores**. **Energy** passes from the grass through the zebra to the lions.

African grasslands are called savannah.

Food chain

Lions watch the zebra, waiting for a chance to attack one

Zebra graze on the grass

Grass grows on an African savannah

Top predators

Lions and hyena are at the top of their **food chains**, because no animal hunts them. **Carnivores** often prey on old, sick or young animals. They pick off the weakest animals, because they are the easiest to catch.

Hyena usually hunt together in clans.

A golden eagle is a top predator and a scavenger in many grasslands.

Hyena and many other **predators** are also **scavengers.** Scavengers feed on dead animals.

Feeding on waste

Scavengers, such as vultures, pick the rotting flesh off dead animals, leaving only clean bones. **Decomposers** go even further.

Vultures wait for the lion to finish her meal, before they feed on the leftovers.

A mushroom has no leaves. It grows from tiny root-like strands in the soil.

Decomposers include mushrooms, worms and many insects. They feed on waste in droppings and the remains of dead plants and animals. As they feed, they break up the waste into tiny pieces, which become part of the soil.

A meadow food chain

Grasslands don't have to be really large. A meadow is a large grassy field. In this **food chain**, **energy** passes from the flowers through the hoverfly to the spider, the lizard and the fox. The fox is an **omnivore** that snatches up the lizard, but also feeds on plants.

This meadow is in Great Britain.

Food chain

The fox pounces on the lizard

The lizard snaps up the spider

The spider catches the hoverfly

The hoverfly finds food in the flower

The flower grows in the meadow

Food webs

The diagram opposite shows how different **food chains** link together to form a **food web.** If all the possibilities were included here, it would include most of the plants and animals in a **habitat!**

Bison feed on shrubs as well as on grass.

Food web

hawk

coyote

black-footed ferret

prairie dog

prairie chicken

bison

cricket

grass and plants

25

Key links

Some animals or plants are particularly important to a **habitat**. Many animals rely on them and they are key links in **food chains**.

A pronghorn likes living close to prairie dogs.

Burrowing owls nest in the prairie dogs' tunnels.

A prairie dog is a key link. Ferrets, golden eagles and hawks hunt prairie dogs. Bison and pronghorn like to graze on grass that has been clipped by prairie dogs.

Protecting food chains

People cause the greatest harm to **food chains**. Huge areas of grasslands are used to grow crops, such as wheat and maize.

Much of the prairie land in North America is used to grow wheat.

Prairie animals are protected in Badlands National Park, USA.

Farmers have killed so many prairie dogs that black-footed ferrets have almost died out. They now survive in national parks, where prairie plants and animals are safe from people.

Glossary

carnivore animal that eats only the meat of other animals

consumer living thing, particularly an animal, that feeds on other living things, such as plants and other animals

decomposer living thing, such as an earthworm, fungus or bacterium, that breaks up the remains of plants and animals and turns them into soil

energy power needed to do something, such as move, breathe or swallow

food chain diagram that shows how energy passes from plants to different animals

food web diagram that shows how different plants and animals in a habitat are linked by what they eat

habitat place where something lives

herbivore animal that eats only plants

omnivore animal that eats plants and animals

predator animal that hunts other animals for food

producer living thing, such as a plant, that makes its own food

scavenger animal that feeds off the flesh and remains of dead animals

Find out more

Books

Food Chains (Cycles in Nature), Theresa Greenaway (Wayland, 2014)

Grassland (Life Cycles), Sean Callery (Kingfisher, 2012)

Grassland Food Chains (Protecting Food Chains), Buffy Silverman (Raintree, 2010)

Who Eats Who in Grasslands? (Food Chains in Action), Moira Butterfield (Franklin Watts, 2009)

Websites

worldwildlife.org/habitats/grasslands
The World Wildlife Fund website has a section on grasslands and the animals that live there.

www.bbc.co.uk/nature/habitats/Tropical_and_subtropical_grasslands,_savannas,_and_shrublands
This BBC website includes videos about several aspects of grasslands and information about many grassland animals.

www.blueplanetbiomes.org/prairie.htm
A website with information about different habitats, or biomes, including the North American prairies.

Index

bison 5, 24, 25, 27

bush 6, 7

carnivores 15, 16, 18, 30

caterpillars 14

cheetahs 9

consumers 14-15, 30

coyotes 15, 25

crickets 25

crops 6, 28

decomposers 20-21, 30

energy 8, 9, 10, 16, 22, 30

ferrets 25, 27, 29

flowers 4, 13, 22, 23

food chains 9, 10-11, 16-17, 18, 22-23, 24, 26, 30

food webs 24-25, 30

foxes 22, 23

golden eagles 19, 27

grass 10, 11, 17, 25

hawks 10, 11, 15, 25, 27

herbivores 14, 16, 30

hoverflies 22, 23

hyena 18, 19

kangaroos 8

key links 26-27

lions 16, 17, 18, 20

lizards 22, 23

meadows 22-23

mushrooms 21

national parks 29

omnivores 15, 22, 30

owls 27

pampas 6, 7

plants 4, 10, 11, 12-13, 14, 15, 17, 28

prairie chickens 25

prairie dogs 10, 11, 14, 25, 26, 27, 29

prairies 6, 7, 10-11, 12

predators 18-19, 30

producers 12, 30

pronghorns 26, 27

protecting food chains 29

savannahs 6, 16-17

scavengers 19, 20, 30

spiders 22, 23

steppes 6, 7

threats to food chains 28

top predators 18-19

vultures 20

zebra 5, 16, 17